SCHOLAS[TIC]
BOOK GUIDES
Cloudy with a Chance of Meatballs

BY JUDI BARRETT

ISBN 0-439-57135-9
Copyright © 2003, 1996 by Scholastic Inc.
All rights reserved.
Printed in the U.S.A.

2 3 4 5 6 7 8 9 10 31 09 08 07 06 05 04 03

NEW YORK • TORONTO • LONDON • AUCKLAND • SYDNEY
MEXICO CITY • NEW DELHI • HONG KONG • BUENOS AIRES

SCHOLASTIC
Teaching
Resources

Contents

Dear Teacher,

Cloudy With a Chance of Meatballs **is a fantastic story about a very unusual community. Students will delight in the detailed, witty illustrations and the clever plot. Through their reading and book conversations, students will come to appreciate this amazing community and the ways in which its citizens solve their problems.**

Overview

TEACHING OPTIONS

There are many ways that students can read and enjoy *Cloudy With a Chance of Meatballs.*

◆ Almost **all students** can benefit from having all or part of the book **read aloud** to help them appreciate the humor in grandpa's tale.

◆ A three-session plan that uses the **key strategy of Compare** and **Contrast** allows for both **teacher guidance** and **demonstrating independence.** This option has students read portions of the book on their own and then participate in teacher-led discussion to stimulate **meaningful conversation** and **comprehension.** See Reading the Book, pages 6–10.

◆ **Cooperative groups** may work together to form **Literature Circles.** A blackline master is provided on page 11 to help students run their own successful Literature Circles.

◆ The blackline master on page 11 may also be adapted for use by students who are reading the book in **pairs** or **independently.**

◆ Introducing the Book, Assess Comprehension, Writing, Activities, and the Story Organizer are features of this guide that may be used with **all students** regardless of the reading options they choose.

JOURNAL WRITING

Students are encouraged to use journal writing to record their observations, note new vocabulary, and express their imaginations. Through journal writing, students are also encouraged to relate what they read to their own lives and to develop the skills to assess their strengths and weaknesses as readers.

Within this guide, **prompts for journal writing** may be found on pages **4, 5, 7, 9, 10, 11, 13,** and **16.**

PORTFOLIO ASSESSMENT

This guide offers a number of opportunities for portfolio assessment of both reading and writing.

WRITING
See pages 13, 14–15, 16.

READING
See pages 12–13, 16.

Introducing the Book

CREATE INTEREST

Ask students to think of their favorite foods. Record their responses on a concept web like the one below. Then ask them to consider what they would do if the foods they loved started to "rain" out of the sky! Tell students that the book they are about to read tells of a very unusual town where this occurrence indeed takes place. In this town knowing tomorrow's weather means that people will know what they are going to eat!

BUILD BACKGROUND

Arrange for students to view a local weather broadcast, either in the classroom, where you or a student become the "weather person"; on videotape; or at home. Before watching, ask students to pay particular attention to the way the forecaster speaks. What words or phrases does he or she repeat? Afterward, tell students that they are about to read a book that uses the same language to describe some very strange weather.

DEVELOP VOCABULARY

Strategy: Context Clues

Explain to students that since *Cloudy With a Chance of Meatballs* has a lot to do with the weather, there are a lot of weather words in it. Read each vocabulary word within the sentence, such as "And now, we have a *prediction* for tomorrow's weather," and invite students to define the word based on the context in which it appears. Reinforce each definition by writing it and the word on the chalkboard.

Personal Word List Encourage students to look for interesting words relating to food or the weather as they read *Cloudy With a Chance of Meatballs*. Suggest that they keep a list of words for each of these categories.

Vocabulary

Organizing Concept: Weather Words

prediction: a statement of what will happen in the future

varied: changed from one time to another

drizzle: light, misty rain

occasional: once in a while

periods: lengths of time with a definite start and finish

gradual: happening slowly

drifts: piles made by the wind

hurricane: A strong storm on the ocean made up of winds moving in a circle

downpour: very heavy rain

tornado: a tall and destructive column of whirling air

PREVIEW AND PREDICT

Determine the Genre Invite students to browse through the book to find out what kind of story it is.

♦ **Is it realistic or a fantasy story? Which type of story has imaginary things, people, or events that could not exist?**

Explore the illustrations Ask students to study the illustrations in the beginning, middle, and end of the book. What changes do you notice in the illustrations? Which illustrations are more realistic?

♦ **In what ways do you think that a story that involves food falling from the sky will be different from other stories you have read?**

Students may record their predictions and questions in their Journals. As they read, they can verify or revise their predictions to see if the book is answering their questions.

ASSESSMENT

As students read the book, notice how they:

✔ make connections with the **theme** of some things changing and some things staying the same in a community.

✔ use the **key strategy of Compare/Contrast**.

✔ recognize how **literary elements and devices**, including Story within a Story and Tall Tale, are developed in *Cloudy With a Chance of Meatballs*.

Reading On Students who are reading the book independently may read at their own pace. Other students may go on to read the first 11 pages of the book, up to the sentence that ends with "in case they got hungry between meals."

Meet the Author and Illustrator

Judi Barrett has written many humorous books for children. Born in Brooklyn, she earned her BFA degree there at the Pratt Institute. Later, she studied Early Childhood Education at Bank Street College. She now teaches art to children and works on new stories in her free time.

Ron Barrett also attended the Pratt Institute and has illustrated many of Judi Barrett's books, including *Cloudy With a Chance of Meatballs,* named an IRA/CBC "Children's Choice." He has worked in advertising and as a consultant to the Children's Television Workshop. He now works as a freelance illustrator in New York City, his birthplace.

MORE BY THE BARRETTS

***Animals Should Definitely Not Act Like People*
by Judi and Ron Barrett**
A series of humorous reversals winds up with a final point about not putting people in cages "because we wouldn't like it."

***Animals Should Definitely Not Wear Clothing*
by Judi and Ron Barrett**
The idea of clothing for animals is explored imaginatively and with great humor.

***Benjamin's 365 Birthdays*
by Judi and Ron Barrett**
Benjamin can't wait another year for his birthday, so he wraps and unwraps familiar objects to make them special.

Reading the Book

This plan is divided into three sessions. Included are mini-lessons on Story within a Story and Tall Tales.

SESSION 1

After the first 11 pages of the book

Synopsis The family is sitting around the breakfast table when Grandpa flips a pancake that flies through the air and lands on Henry's head. Prompted by the pancake incident, Grandpa tells a "tall-tale bedtime story" about a town called Chewandswallow. There are no grocery stores in Chewandswallow. All of the food the people need comes from the sky. They watch weather reports on television to find out what they will eat and they carry plates, cups, glasses and utensils so they will be prepared for any kind of weather.

 LAUNCH THE KEY STRATEGY

COMPARE/CONTRAST

THINK ALOUD **When you compare things, you look at ways in which they are alike. When you contrast things, you look at ways in which they are different. For example, I see that the town of Chewandswallow is like other towns in many ways, but there is one big difference. The people in Chewandswallow get their food from the sky instead of from a store. As I continue to read I will look for more ways to compare and contrast information about characters, events, and setting to help me understand the story.**

COMPREHENSION CHECK

What did you like best about this part of the book? Why? (Respond to Literature)

How is the family shown in the beginning of the book like the people of Chewandswallow? How are they different? (Key Strategy: Compare/Contrast) *They are alike in most ways. They live in similar houses and have cats and dogs. They are different in the way they get their food.*

What happened to Henry and his sister on Saturday? Tell the events in order. (Sequence) *The children were discussing how many pancakes they could eat. Grandpa flipped a pancake. The pancake flew through the air and landed on Henry's head. That night, Grandpa told a story about a town where food comes out of the sky.*

Why do the illustrations show the children listening to their grandfather on one side of the page and the world spread out in a big picture behind them? (Distinguish Between Fantasy/Reality) *The illustration shows what the children are imagining as their grandfather tells the story.*

Do the children like listening to their grandfather's story? How do you know? (Draw Conclusions) *They do, because they describe it as the "best" story he has ever told, and the illustration shows them paying attention and smiling as he talks.*

Would it be a good or a bad thing to have food come from the sky? Why? (Make Judgments) *Possible answers: It's a good thing, because you would never have to go shopping or cook; the food doesn't cost money; you can eat outdoors. It would not be a good thing, because you could get messy or hurt from falling food; the food might go bad and make people sick; you might not like the day's selections; people would fail to use manners.*

What do you think will happen in the town of Chewandswallow? (Make, Confirm, Revise Predictions) *Answers should contain references to the possible consequences of food coming from the sky.*

 Who tells you stories? What kinds of stories do you like to hear most? Tell about your favorite stories and how you heard them.

Reading On On the next ten pages of the book, we learn more about the weather in Chewandswallow and its effect on the people who live there. Ask students to predict what problems might happen when the weather changes.

EXTRA HELP The illustrations in this book provide strong contextual support. To assist students in predicting vocabulary and meaning in the text, have them preview the illustrations before reading and discuss with a partner what appears to be happening in each one. **(Use Visuals)**

ACCESS Pair auditory learners and students who require additional reading support with other students, who will read the story aloud to them. After listening and/or following along with their books, ask the students to retell the story in their own words. Encourage students to participate in book discussions and respond to guided questioning. **(Retell)**

Reading the Book

Synopsis Different foods fall upon Chewandswallow each day. Breakfast foods fall in the morning, lunch foods at midday and dinner foods fall in the evening. The Sanitation Department cleans up after every meal. Everyone is happy until they start getting some bad weather. One day so much spaghetti falls that it ties up traffic. On other days the town is pelted with smelly Gorgonzola cheese all day long, overcooked broccoli, thick pea soup fog. Storms of giant pancakes and jelly sanwiches make things worse. There is even a tomato tornado!

COMPREHENSION CHECK

Would you like to live in Chewandswallow? Why or why not? (Respond to Literature)

Could this story about Chewandswallow be a separate story on its own or do we need the beginning when the children are having breakfast with Grandpa? (Story within a Story) *Possible answers: The story could stand on its own. Why? Grandpa and the children don't come into the story that he tells. It does help to read about the breakfast, because we meet Grandpa and therefore find the story more interesting.* `MINI-LESSON`

MINI-LESSON

AUTHOR'S CRAFT: STORY WITHIN A STORY

TEACH/MODEL Point out that *Cloudy With a Chance of Meatballs* is a *story within a story*. The story about Chewandswallow is within another story about a family that begins with them eating pancakes. Discuss why the author chose to write her book in this way.

APPLY Invite students to use a chart like the one on this page to make note of differences between the "outside" story and the "inside" story, as seen in both the text and the illustrations.

Story Elements	Outside Story	Inside Story
Who Is Telling the Story?	Henry's Sister	Grandpa
Setting	a realistic home	fantasy town where food falls from the sky
Events	eats pancakes cooked in kitchen listen to a story	eat food from the sky Sanitation crew cleans leftovers

How is the weather in Chewandswallow different from the way it was before? How is it still the same? (Key Strategy: Compare/Contrast) *It is different in that the food is getting big and dangerous. People are no longer happy. It is the same in that food is still falling from the sky instead of rain or snow.*

How do the details in the illustrations help readers understand the problems the change in the weather is causing? What details shown in the pictures present the biggest problems? (Illustrators Craft) *Answers will vary. Possible answers: One day Gorgonzola cheese fell from the sky all day long; one day there was a pea soup fog and no one could see where they were going; when there was a storm of pancakes one morning, a huge pancake covered the school.*

How is the food weather made to seem believable? (Author's Craft: Humor) *Grandpa talks about it as if it was an everyday thing, and even uses weather report words to talk about it.*

 What would be your favorite meal if you lived in the town of Chewandswallow? Write about it in your Journal.

Reading On Invite students to read on to discover what happens to the people of Chewandswallow and how the book ends.

SUPPORTING ·ALL LEARNERS

EXTRA HELP For additional practice with cause and effect relationships and to extend higher level thinking, have students work together to make a small model or diorama of the town of Chewandswallow in crises. Encourage students to come up with an original storm and to show the havoc that kind of storm would wreak. **(Hands On)**

CHALLENGE The illustrator, Ron Barrett, created an unusual truck to solve the sanitation problems of Chewandswallow. Challenge students to design other inventions that would solve the unique problems that might occur in this town. Suggest that students study the illustrations for clues for problems to solve. Students may want to share their ideas with other students on the Bulletin Board. **(Innovate)**

Reading the Book

Synopsis The weather in Chewandswallow becomes so bad that the Sanitation Department can no longer handle it. The school must be closed when it is covered by a giant pancake, and everyone fears for their lives. The people of Chewandswallow decide to abandon the town. They glue stale bread together to make rafts and sail to a new land. After sailing for a week, a coastal town welcomes them. They use the bread to create temporary shelters and gradually become adjusted to their new lives. Grandpa completes his story and kisses the children good night. When the children go sledding the next day, they imagine that the sun over the snow-covered hill is a giant pat of butter on a mound of mashed potatoes.

COMPREHENSION CHECK

What do you think is the most surprising thing that happened in this part of the book ? (Respond to Literature)

The illustration of the town becoming covered with food includes the words "Look Out!" spelled out by alphabet soup. What other visual jokes can you find on this page? (Illustrator's Craft: Details) *Possible answers: one man has a big piece of tube shaped pasta on his head, and giant donuts are rolling down the street.*

Could people really make a raft out of stale bread? What does this tell you about the tall tale Grandpa is telling? (Tall Tale) *The girl who is narrating the story says that Grandpa is telling a tall tale. In tall tales impossible things happen and the characters act as if these things are normal.* `MINI-LESSON`

Why do the people of Chewandswallow feel they must leave their town? (Cause/Effect) *It's not safe— they could be seriously hurt from falling food.*

What is different about the new country the people of Chewandswallow come to? (Key Strategy: Compare/Contrast) *They have to get used to buying food in a store and cooking it.*

 Was the snowy hill that Henry and his sister saw really a mountain of mashed potatoes? Write your own tall tale about it.

MINI-LESSON

TALL TALE

TEACH/MODEL The children in the story call Grandpa's story a "tall tale." Tell students that many favorite American stories, such as the stories about Paul Bunyan or Davy Crockett, or weather so hot that all the corn in the field popped before it could be harvested, are called tall tales. These are stories in which something, or a series of things, happens that is completely impossible but is presented by the teller with credibility, such as sailing away on a raft of stale bread. These stories are usually funny, as is *Cloudy With a Chance of Meatballs.*

APPLY Invite students to note more details that are both humorous and impossible.

Literature Circles

Use these cards to help you as you read and discuss *Cloudy With A Chance of Meatballs.* Record your ideas and answers in your Journal as you read.

S E S S I O N
First eleven pages

TALK ABOUT IT What do you learn about the girl and her brother from the words and illustrations in this part of the story? What did you learn about Grandpa? Would you have believed Grandpa's story? Why or why not? Do you need to believe it to be able to enjoy it? Discuss your answers with your group.

S E S S I O N
Next ten pages

TALK ABOUT IT What parts of this story do you think are funny? Why? Write your ideas and share them with the group. Then with the group, discuss the different ways the author and illustrator make the story funny. Which do you enjoy the most in the book—the story or the illustrations? Why?

S E S S I O N
Final nine pages

TALK ABOUT IT What would the people of your town or city have done to welcome the people of Chewandswallow? With the others, discuss how you think the adults and the children got used to life in their new town. What things would be easy? What would be difficult?

Assess Comprehension

REFLECT AND RESPOND

How did the community of Chewandswallow change? How did it stay the same?
(✔ Theme Connection)

How is the town of Chewandswallow like your town? How is it different?
(✔ Key Strategy: Compare/Contrast)

How would the story be different if the author told the story directly, without the children and Grandpa at the beginning and end?
(✔ Literary Device: Story-within-a-story)

What kinds of unusual weather can you imagine to add to the tall tale part of this story?
(✔ Tall Tale)

STORY ORGANIZER

Copy and distribute the Story Organizer on page 16 of this guide. Invite students to complete this page on their own. Encourage them to share their completed work by comparing their answers with those of other students.

READ CRITICALLY ACROSS TEXTS

On the Day Peter Stuyvesant Sailed into Town

◆ If Peter Stuyvesant had sailed into Chewandswallow, what would have been his reaction? How might he have helped them deal with the bad weather? Would he have been successful?

Just a Dream

◆ Walter and the people of Chewandswallow encounter problems. Looking just at the pictures in both books, how do the details in each contribute to your understanding of the story? Which pictures do you like better? Why?

Mary McLeod Bethune

◆ The communities in both books must solve problems. Which problems are the most difficult to solve? Why? Which problems are most like the problems in your community?

A Topic for Conversation

NEW SOLUTIONS

People must deal with many problems in books and in real life. In *Cloudy With a Chance of Meatballs*, Judi Barrett writes humorously about a town with a pretty serious problem. They solve it by sailing away. Sometimes problems can't just be sailed away from. Should they have stayed and tried to solve their problem? Or dealt with it in another way? Invite all those who have read *Cloudy With a Chance of Meatballs* to discuss this question.

POSSIBLE ANSWERS:

Sailing away was the best thing to do. No one can control the weather, and their town was being destroyed.

They could have stayed and changed their way of life. If they lived underground or in specially strong houses the weather wouldn't affect them.

They should have invented new ways to deal with the weather. No one can tell what they could have done if they had tried.

They should have asked for help. People from other places could have sent special equipment and emergency supplies.

They should have waited. Just like a drought or a spell of some other kind of bad weather, their weather would probably have improved if they had waited.

IDEA FILE

Vocabulary

There are many words relating to the weather in *Cloudy With a Chance of Meatballs*. Invite students to revisit the book and their word lists and use those words to write a weather report. It could be a realistic report or a tall tale.

Ask the Illustrator

What would students like to ask Ron Barrett about the artwork in *Cloudy With a Chance of Meatballs*? They might be interested to know how he imagined something that doesn't exist. Encourage students to write their ideas and questions in their Journals.

Reviews by You

Many people think *Cloudy With a Chance of Meatballs* is a funny book. Encourage students to write their own reviews of the book, saying what they liked most about it, and whether or not they think it is funny and why.

Describe a Beautiful Day

Invite children to use their favorite foods to plan a day of beautiful weather for Chewandswallow. They can write their description in the form of a paragraph or as a script for a weather report. Students may wish to add illustrations to their written descriptions.

Stories About the Weather For as long as we can remember, people have used stories to explain the weather. The Cherokee Indians told stories in which their Sun God, dressed in golden robes, drove away storms. He rode on a swift eagle, moving so fast that the multicolored hem of his robe was spread out behind him from the tip of one eagle wing to the other in a huge semicircle. This made a rainbow.

ASSESSMENT

The checked questions on page 12 help assess students' understanding of:

✔ the **theme** of things changing and things staying the same in a community.

✔ the **key strategy of Compare/Contrast**.

✔ how the author uses literary elements such as **Story Within a Story** and **Tall Tale.**

You may also wish to review and discuss selected students' completed Story Organizers.

Listen to Students Read Ask selected students to read aloud from a part of the book where the author's message about life is clear. You may wish to tape-record students as they read the section aloud.

Students may add their recordings, copies of favorite journal entries, their completed Story Organizer, and other completed assignments to their Literacy Portfolios.

Writing

WRITING PROMPTS

Writer's Style: Tall Tale

Judi Barrett imagines an impossible situation, weather that is made up of food and drink, and then writes about it as if it were an everyday thing. Invite students to imagine their own impossible situation or thing. What is it? Where and when does it happen? How are people's lives affected by it? Suggest that they write about it as if it were an everyday part of life that everyone in their story accepts as normal. When they revise, encourage them to check that their tall tales describe the impossible thing as if it were a normal, typical occurrence, not as if it were amazing and fantastic.

Diary Entry

People go about their lives in Chewandswallow much like we do, with the only significant difference being the food and drink that falls from the sky. Invite students to revisit the book and select incidents to include in a diary entry written by someone living in or visiting the town. They could choose a normal day or a day on which the weather got worse. Encourage students to incorporate vocabulary words and words from their personal word lists. When they revise, remind students to use words that appeal to the five senses so that readers can visualize what they are describing.

Newspaper Article

Have students turn to the page with the picture of The Chewandswallow Digest and reread the headlines. Invite them to imagine another event occurring in Chewandswallow, on which they may report. As they write the article, they should remember that the first sentence should make people want to read more. Also use a chart like the one below to help them remember that a good article answers who? what? when? where? why? and how?. After they have completed the article, they will need to write a snappy headline for it, perhaps making a joke with wording. Students can then publish their articles in a "special edition" of The Chewandswallow Digest.

Headline: _____					
Who?	**What?**	**When?**	**Where?**	**Why?**	**How?**

Activities

INTEGRATING LANGUAGE ARTS

Reading/Writing/Speaking

And Now for the Weather Suggest to students that they write a daily weather forecast for the town of Chewandswallow. First, they will need to reread the pages of the book in which Judi Barrett describes the weather in Chewandswallow. They should listen to a weather forecaster on television, and jot down some of the words frequently used. They can then plan one day's "menu" for Chewandswallow—what will come from the sky for breakfast, lunch, and dinner. This should then be written out into a weather report. Students may wish to draw a map to show listeners what the weather will be like that day. They can practice and present their weather forecast to their classmates.

Speaking/Listening/Viewing

Survey Invite students to work in pairs to discover which food from the book *Cloudy With a Chance of Meatballs* is most popular with their classmates. Students can go back to the book to select five foods that fell from the sky. Then have them ask their classmates which of the foods they like best. Ask students to create bar graphs to summarize their findings. Next students can work together to create word problems based on the information in their graphs. Enourage them to share their graphs with the class and challenge others to use the graphs to answer their word problems.

INTEGRATING THE CURRICULUM

Science

Track the Weather In *Cloudy With a Chance of Meatballs* the weather changed drastically all day long. Weather usually changes throughout the day— even if it's not in such obvious ways. Working in small groups, one to each activity, or as a class, students can track the changing weather in your location. Possible activities include: 1. Take the temperature every hour during one day and make a graph to show the findings. 2. Go outdoors in the morning, afternoon and early evening to look at the clouds. Sketch the sky at the different times of day to remember how the sky changes.

Art

Foodscapes After Grandpa tells the story of Chewandswallow, the children imagine that their own backyard looks like mashed potatoes with butter. Invite students to think about the scenery around your home or school. What food does it look like? Suggest that they draw a picture of the scenery so that it looks like food. For instance, a student might draw a tree to look like a broccoli stalk or a rock that looks like a cinnamon bun. Students' drawings can be posted for others to see, or combined into a class book of foodscapes.

Story Organizer

Use the diagram below to compare and contrast life in Chewandswallow in the beginning of the story with the way it was after the weather turned stormy.

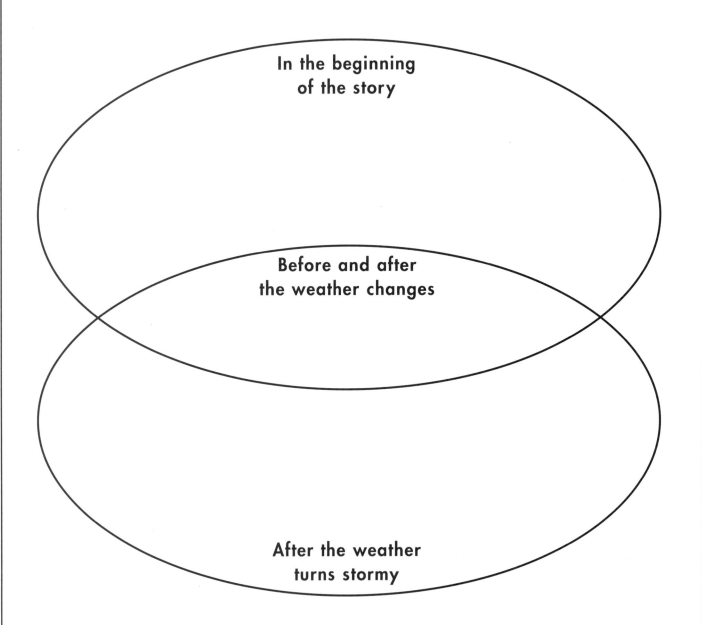

**In the beginning
of the story**

**Before and after
the weather changes**

**After the weather
turns stormy**

How is your community the same in good weather and bad? How is it different?